BOOK

CW00674581

Written by
 Translated by Emma Lunt

The First Man
BY ALBERT CAMUS

Bright
≡Summaries.com

ALBERT CAMUS

FRENCH WRITER, PLAYWRIGHT, ESSAYIST AND PHILOSOPHER

- **Born in Mondovi (Algeria) in 1913**
- **Died in Villeblevin (France) in 1960**
- **Notable works:**
  - *The Stranger* (1942), novel
  - *The Myth of Sisyphus* (1942), essay
  - *The Plague* (1947), novel

Albert Camus (1913-1960), a Frenchman born in Algeria and the winner of a Nobel Prize in Literature, was one of the major writers of the 20th century. He was a profoundly committed intellectual, a philosopher, a journalist, a playwright and a novelist, and left his mark through his reflection on the Absurd, which found a nuanced, sensitive and humanist expression in his work.

Camus, who was widely admired and sometimes criticised, resonated considerably across the world with his novels *The Plague* (1947) and, above all, *The Stranger* (1942). He died prematurely in 1960 following a car accident.

THE FIRST MAN

A CHILD IN SEARCH OF AN ABSENT FATHER

- **Genre:** autobiographical novel
- **Reference edition:** Camus, A. (2013) *The First Man*. Trans. Hapgood, D. London: Penguin UK.
- **First edition:** 1994
- **Themes:** memory, family, identity, death, Algeria

The First Man is an unfinished autobiographical novel. Published by Albert Camus' daughter through the French publishing company *Éditions Gallimard* in 1994, this work should have been the first part of a trilogy. In it, the author recounts, through his alter ego Jacques Cormery, his childhood in a small village in Algeria with his mother and grandmother, his adult life in France, as well as his attempts to find out what type of man his father had been.

SUMMARY

The novel begins with a dedication to the author's mother: "To you who will never be able to read this".

A couple, including a pregnant woman, arrive in a cart driven by an Arab in the village of Solférino, in the highlands of Algeria, not far from the Tunisian border. The father has just taken ownership of some land there. They have not yet entered the farm when the woman begins to feel the first contractions. While her husband goes to find a doctor, she is taken care of by some Arab women. When the practitioner and her husband arrive, she has already given birth. The child is none other than the hero of the story, Jacques Cormery, the author's double. Unfortunately, the child's father dies in combat a few years after his birth, during the First World War. Jacques has very few memories of him. The only significant event that he really remembers is the execution of Pirette, a murderer, which his father attended. Jacques remembers him returning to the house and what he had said. This story affected him to such a degree that he feels as though he went with his father.

Forty years later, Jacques travels by train from Paris to Saint-Brieuc. At his mother's request, he visits the cemetery to see his father's grave. For him this visit is meaningless, as his father is like a stranger. It is only because one of his friends has retired to the town and he wishes to visit him that he decides to visit the cemetery. Upon finding the dates on the tombstone, he is shaken: his father died when he was younger than Jacques himself. This drives him to research the man who gave him life. This investigation into his father's past allows him to recount his story and to talk about his family.

Jacques has dinner with a friend, Victor Malan, whom he profoundly admires. This man seems to be like a father to him. Jacques discloses to him his project of searching for information about his father, but Victor fears that he will be disappointed. Despite this warning, Jacques is convinced that he must do this research and decides to leave for Algeria. This return to his past makes it clear to him that the darkness in him is due to the silence of his family and his people. In fact, over the course of the story, the author shows the contrast between the land of Algeria, where sandstorms clear all memories, and Metropolitan France, which preserves memories. Furthermore, Jacques' family were extremely poor and, according to him, the poor have fewer temporal and spatial markers than the rich.

The matriarch of the family was his grandmother, so it is not surprising that Jacques describes her in detail. An authoritative figure, she is the one who managed the money, bought clothes and groceries, and ran all the family's activities. She showed no tenderness. On the boat that takes him to Algeria, Jacques remembers the siestas he took with her in the apartment in Algiers: when it was too hot, his grandmother forced him to sleep with her, and for him these siestas were times of great boredom. He also remembers that one day his grandmother had asked him to go and find a chicken to eat in the chicken coop. Despite his fear, he had performed the task. To thank him for his bravery, his grandmother had invited him to help in the kitchen while its throat was being slit. Watching this spectacle, Jacques had been overcome by a phobia of death.

Jacques visits his mother. She seems "gentle, polite, complaisant, even passive [...] isolated by her semideafness", in total contrast to Jacques' grandmother. He asks her about his father, but Lucie Cormery remembers only a few things: her memories are limited to around the mayor's announcement of her husband's death and being given back the piece of shrapnel that had fatally injured him. In the street, an explosion reverberates, reminding them that they are in the heart of the Algerian War. In fact, the narration is set in 1954.

Étienne is Jacques' uncle. He is very handsome, but was even more deaf than Lucie, to the point that he had been unable to work during his childhood. He had therefore taken the opportunity to learn to read. Jacques remembers hunting expeditions with him and his dog Brillant. The author recounts his uncle's rages were "as immediate and wholehearted as his pleasures". He had been Jacques' first male role model.

Jacques then talks about M. Bernard, his school teacher, who had also been a surrogate father for him. He had fought in the Battle of the Marne and made it home. The parallel between him and Jacques' father was therefore very clear. The author describes the development of the class and the privileged relationship he shared with his teacher. While M. Bernard was full of affection for the students, he was no less strict because of this: when the children made a serious mistake, he gave them a whipping with a large ruler that he called the "sugar cane". This punishment was accepted by the students as the teacher was completely fair. At the time, it was primarily up to teachers to instil moral values.

At the end of the year, M. Bernard had signed Jacques up for a scholarship for sixth forms and colleges, and thus the young Cormery had been able to continue his studies, despite his family's poverty.

M. Bernard's students who had succeeded at continuing their studies realised that they were henceforth left to themselves. When Jacques had had to write down his mother's profession on a document at the start of the year he, encouraged by a fellow student, had written "housemaid". This is when he began to feel ashamed and became aware of the importance of parents in constructing your own identity.

Thursdays, when he wasn't in detention, and Sundays were dedicated to grocery shopping and working in the house. The rest of the time, Jacques played football with his friends on the beach. The teams were composed of Arabs and French people. Sometimes, he went to read picture books and stories about heroes at the local library. Jacques had a passion for reading. He often won books during prize-giving at school.

At the end of the story, he has not found all of the answers he was looking for, but he holds on to the feelings and memories of his family, his youth and of his mother who he loved dearly.

CHARACTER STUDY

JACQUES CORMERY

Jacques Cormery, the narrator, is the double of Albert Camus, the author.

The novel is based on the parallel between Jacques as a child and Jacques as an adult. The latter remembers the first, and Jacques is in constant oscillation between the two characters. Raised without a father, Jacques grows up in a very poor family in Algiers. He dearly loves his mother and fears his grandmother. He is an obedient boy. Talented at school, he pursues his studies at college, and benefits from the teaching and culture that the rest of his family missed out on.

Once he is an adult, he goes to his father's grave in Saint-Brieuc. The episode triggers his desire to research his father and is the driving force behind the story – perhaps even the reason the novel was written. This research takes place fairly late: Jacques is already 40 years old. According to him, men's personalities are shaped thanks to their parents. Jacques therefore begins a true journey of self-discovery through researching his father.

LUCIE CORMERY

Lucie Cormery is the mother of Jacques and Louis (who is sometimes called Henri in the novel). Rarely called by her first name, she is often referred to by her role, her place in the family: his mother. The visits of Antoine, her suitor, are the only times when she is presented as a woman before anything else.

The novel is dedicated to her: "To you who will never be able to read this". Indeed, Lucie Cormery, who is very poor, never had access to education and does not know how to read. Furthermore, her deafness confines her, isolates her and condemns her to a contemplative attitude. The author writes that she "gaze[s] once more out of the same window and watch[es] the activity on the same street that she had been contemplating through half her lifetime". Her state of withdrawal forces her to give up her role in educating her children to her mother, who is the family matriarch. From then on, Lucie is a mother, not because she educates her children, but because of the love she gives them.

HENRI CORMERY

Henri Cormery is Jacques' father. Like his wife, he is rarely called by his first name. Designated by the generic term "the man", he takes on a general, almost parabolic dimension. He appears in the first chapter, at Jacques' birth. He was born in 1885 and dies in 1914 in Saint-Brieuc, after being injured in the Battle of the Marne. This father, who has died and been forgotten on unknown territory (Metropolitan France), acts as the driving force behind the story. Jacques, having seen his grave at the Saint-Brieuc cemetery, will not stop searching for information about this stranger that gave him life.

THE GRANDMOTHER

The grandmother is not referred to by her name, but, as with Lucie Cormery, and to a greater extent, she is defined by her role: she is the head of the family. She manages the money, the work and the distribution of household chores. She is the one who decides whether Jacques should continue his studies and she is also the one who finds him a job at a ship-broker's. Unlike her daughter, who is full of love and gentleness, the grandmother is exclusively a figure of authority and punishment. The education of Jacques and Louis is therefore divided in two: their mother brings love and affection, while their grandmother shows strictness, instilling in them a certain discipline. Jacques never shows affection towards her, and her death is not even given a paragraph in the novel.

ÉTIENNE

Étienne is the uncle of Jacques and Louis. Despite his position as the only man of the family, he does not have a significant role in Jacques' education. Affected by an even more severe level of deafness than his sister Lucie, he was not able to work during his childhood, which allowed him to learn to read. This character is the sole subject of a long chapter in the novel, in which Jacques builds up a portrait of him and describes their relationship.

M. BERNARD

M. Bernard is Jacques' schoolteacher. He is also the boy's

surrogate father: "This man [Jacques] had never known his father, but he often spoke to [M. Bernard] of him in a rather mythological way, and in any case at a critical time he knew how to take the father's role"; "I [M. Bernard] fought the war with their fathers and I survived. I try at least here to take the place of my dead comrades". M. Bernard fought in the Battle of the Marne, like Henri Cormery, but he returned. It is thanks to him that Jacques shapes his identity, that he goes to college and undoubtedly that he became a writer.

M. Bernard is also the one and only means of remembering. He thus contrasts with the erased memory that is omnipresent throughout the novel. It is thanks to him that Jacques succeeds in retracing his story, particularly through reading a novel in class about the First World War, *Les Croix de Bois* (*Wooden Crosses*) by Dorgelès, which is a bit like his own father's story.

ANALYSIS

THE ALGERIAN POPULATION

The population is, by definition, a grouping of people, taken collectively, whose individuality is taken away and who are therefore anonymous. Having grown up in a poor family in Algiers, Jacques Cormery/Albert Camus succeeded in escaping this anonymity ("He had tried to escape from anonymity, from a life that was poor, ignorant and mulish; he could not live that life of blind patience, without words, with no thought beyond the present"), unlike his loved ones. He wishes from then on to give a name and a voice to the people that made him who he is:

- On the one hand, he does this by embodying his people in certain characters, particularly that of his mother. Indeed, who better represents these anonymous people, silent and without memory, this land of forgetting that is Algeria, than his unassuming mother, who is without memories and withdrawn into mutism? The mother, a representation of the Algerian people, therefore takes on an allegorical dimension.
- On the other hand, by retelling his own memories, Jacques places the people in the background of his novel. Consequently, by writing, he gives their story back to them, gives them a voice and thus recreates a past for them. The novel thus represents the vox populi (the voice of the people). This is defined as "a single anonymous shadow [that] would sometimes emerge, accompanied by soft footsteps and the indistinct sound of voices". A

true homage to the people, *The First Man* is the voice of the people about the people.

The author emphasises the fact that the Algerian population is without memory, and that they live only in the present, not in the past nor the future: "an enormous oblivion spread over them [the people]". This lack of memory of the people is explained by Camus in a very concrete way: "poor people's memory is less nourished than that of the rich; it has fewer landmarks in space because they seldom leave the place where they live, and fewer reference points in time throughout lives that are grey and featureless".

The fear of forgetting is also one of the motivations behind the novel. Thus, it is because Albert Camus does not want his story and that of his people to be forgotten that he writes. He wants to keep a trace of his family, his origins and, above all, his father.

MEMORY AND HISTORY

History and memory hold a very important place in this autobiographical novel. And therein lies the paradox, as it deals with the story of a man who does not have a history and memories in a family without memory, as we have explained above.

Two stories seem to coexist in the novel, that of Algiers and that of Metropolitan France. The land of Algiers is without memory, while France preserves its memories. These two lands, whose presence alternates in the novel, are very distinct in the author's mind and are extremely different:

"The Mediterranean separates two worlds in me, one where memories and names are preserved in measured spaces, the other where the wind and sand erase all trace of me on the open ranges", the narrator explains. There is, on the one hand, the land where he was a child, namely Algeria, and on the other hand, the land of the adult that he is and that remembers: France. During his research, Jacques returns to the farm where he was born; there, he speaks to a farmer who lives there now and that says to him "Since you're from here, you know how it is. We don't preserve anything here. We tear down and we rebuild. We think about the future and forget the rest". This contrast between the two lands is evident thanks to the example of the graves: the worn out and plant-covered graves at the Mondovi cemetery contrast, of course, with those in Saint-Brieuc.

Two characters who meant a lot to Jacques and who were essential in his education are very representative of the opposition between the two lands. The first, Lucie Cormery, represents forgetting, the land of Algiers and poverty, as we have already said; the other, M. Bernard, acts as a portal to memory and a link to Metropolitan France. Lucie Cormery does not have any memories; she is condemned to forgetting. Thus, to the questions that Jacques poses, she constantly responds that she does not remember or that she has never known. M. Bernard, for his part, tries, through culture and teaching, to give Jacques a history, which is not his own, but which could be. Reading the book *Les Croix de bois*, it is not his father's war story, but it could have been. M. Bernard is the one who makes the link with Metropolitan France and gives the young boy his first reference points.

Thus, the novel's title is clarified: the 'first man' refers to Jacques, who was born in an ex nihilo (meaning *out of nothing*) land (Algeria) and who therefore does not manage to rebuild his story through memory. Despite all his research, many doubts remain amongst his memories. He is the first man not only because the history of Algeria fell into oblivion before him, but also because by recounting his story, he becomes the representative of all the men of Algeria.

THE THEMES OF SUN AND EXOTICISM

The theme of sun is recurrent in Camus' works. It is present in *The Stranger*, for example, where the sun plays an active role in the development of the action. In *The First Man*, the sun is more discreet, but is no less omnipresent. It has many roles and many meanings:

- It is, above all, a synonym for Jacques' suffocation and boredom. The heat of the sun reminds him of his childhood siestas: when the sun was too hot, his grandmother forced him to have a siesta with her, during which he was very bored. Thus, the siestas were preceded by young Jacques' words: "I'm bored! I'm bored!" repeated "like a litany".
- Then, the sun accompanies Jacques in his memories: it is thanks to the sun that he manages to remember Algiers. In fact, for Jacques, one does not exist without the other: the sun is closely linked to the town of Algiers. The sun gives off debilitating heat, which seems to be the recurring atmosphere in the town. Furthermore, in Chapter 4, on the boat that leads him to Algiers, the sun accompanies

him. It is like a common thread in his memories that leads him to the land of his childhood.

- Finally, the sun exacerbates violence. During Jacques' visit to Solférino, in the farm where he was born, he meets the doctor who had been there at his birth. The doctor tells him, referring to the Algerians' resistance to colonialism, that since the days of Cain, the first criminal, men have been terrible and that they are worst under the blazing sun. Violence is, in part, justified by the sun.

The Algerian sun contrasts with the coldness of Metropolitan France. For young Jacques, who knows only great heat and arid landscapes, the freezing coldness of France is mythical. He recounts that stories of children wearing bonnets and woollen scarves on snow-covered paths were truly exotic for him. These stories, told in class, were for him part of the powerful poetry of school and fed his dreams. This positive exoticism was overtaken in his imagination by negative exoticism, where "fear and menace prowled". In fact, he also associated Metropolitan France with the war, because his father had left for France to fight.

FURTHER REFLECTION

SOME QUESTIONS TO THINK ABOUT...

- In what way could we say that *The First Man* is a novel about history and memory? How is it paradoxical to say that?
- What place does fantasy hold in Albert Camus' work?
- How can the first chapter be likened to a story of a Biblical birth? What effect does this have?
- Camus wanted, throughout his life, to speak in the name of those whose voice had been refused. In *The First Man*, this desire of the author is also present. Explain this.
- Is the poverty in Albert Camus' novel a real hindrance to freedom? If yes, why?
- Study the place and representation of the population in the novel.
- Can we say that *The First Man* is an initiation novel?
- What role does the sun play in the work? Compare this to its role in Camus' other works such as *The Stranger* or *Noces*.
- What reasons do you think drove Albert Camus to dedicate the novel to his mother?

We want to hear from you!
Leave a comment on your online library
and share your favourite books on social media!

FURTHER READING

REFERENCE EDITION

- Camus, A. (2013) *The First Man*. Trans. Hapgood, D. London: Penguin UK.

ADAPTATIONS

- *The First Man*. (2011) [Film]. Gianni Amelio. Dir. France/Italy: Cattleya.

MORE FROM BRIGHTSUMMARIES.COM

- *The Fall* by Albert Camus (Book Analysis)
- *The Just Assassins* by Albert Camus (Book Analysis)
- *The Myth of Sisyphus* by Albert Camus (Book Analysis)
- *The Plague* by Albert Camus (Book Analysis)
- *The Stranger* by Albert Camus (Book Analysis)

Printed in Great Britain
by Amazon

59381755R00016